WORSHIP

Touching the heart of God

SELWYN HUGHES AND
PHILIP GREENSLADE

WORSHIP

Touching the heart of God

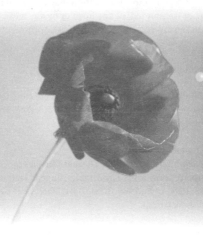

Copyright © CWR 2004

First published by CWR as *Every Day with Jesus, A Fresh Vision for Worship*, September/October 2003.

This new revised edition published 2004 by CWR, Waverley Abbey House, Waverley Lane, Farnham, Surrey GU9 8EP, England.

The right of Selwyn Hughes and Philip Greenslade to be identified as the authors of this work has been asserted by them in accordance with the Copyright, Designs and Patents Act 1988, sections 77 and 78.

See back of book for list of National Distributors.

Unless otherwise indicated, all Scripture references are from the Holy Bible: New International Version (NIV), copyright © 1973, 1978, 1984 by the International Bible Society.

Other Scripture quotations are marked:
NKJV: *New King James Version*, © 1982, Thomas Nelson Inc.
The Message: Scripture taken from *The Message*, Eugene Peterson. Copyright © 1993, 1994, 1995, 1996, 2000, 2001, 2002. Used by permission of NavPress Publishing Group.

Concept development, editing, design and production by CWR

Cover image: Carol Sharp/Flowerphotos.com

Printed in Slovenia by Compass Press

ISBN: 1-85345-341-2

CONTENTS

INTRODUCTION

No greater theme could ever occupy our attention than the one we are about to consider: *the worship of God*. A.W. Tozer, writing in the early part of the last century, said, 'Worship is the missing jewel of the evangelical church.' In some ways things have changed since Tozer wrote those striking words for over the past decades the Holy Spirit has been renewing His Church in a wonderful way and bringing Christians of all denominations to a new understanding of the meaning of worship. However, there is still much to learn if we are to plumb the depths of this vitally important subject.

Recorded in Revelation 5, the apostle John catches a glimpse of the worship being offered in heaven – the kind of worship, we suggest, that should be offered on earth. When we cry from the depth of our beings and with the utmost sincerity, 'Worthy is the Lamb', then we come near to the heart of worship. 'Worship' is to ascribe 'worth' to what we value the most, and no one is more worthy of our adoration and praise than the one Creator God Himself. The more we contemplate the majesty of God the more we are drawn to Him. When we are moved by a magnificent sunset or by a field of beautiful flowers our natural response is to gasp, 'Oh, how beautiful'. How much greater, then, should be our response when we consider who God is and what He does.

In his letter to the Romans Paul pours out his feelings after reflecting on the riches of God's grace. For a moment he pauses in worship and then he exclaims, 'Oh, the depth of the riches of the wisdom and knowledge of God!' (Rom. 11:33). Amazement and wonder are always the natural response to the contemplation of God's mercy and grace.

CHAPTER ONE

THE HEART OF WORSHIP

Romans 12:1–8
Ephesians 1:3–14

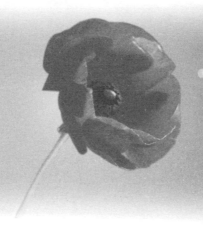

*'Worthy is the Lamb, who was slain, to receive
… honour and glory and praise!'*
Revelation 5:12

It may be argued that there is a subtle difference between worship and praise. Some say we *praise* God for what He does and we *worship* Him for who He is. In this book, however, the term 'worship' is being used in its broadest sense to describe our heartfelt response to God and His goodness. That response may be praise, thanksgiving, blessing, service, or even, as we shall see, lament.

In Romans 12, Paul describes worship as the offering of our *whole selves* as a living sacrifice to God. Worship involves our response to God not only when we go to church on a Sunday but also in what we do from Monday to Saturday. What happens when worshippers gather together on a Sunday is meant to be the concentration, the summing-up and focus of what all life is about. Nowadays there is a tendency in many churches to regard praise and worship as something that is done at the beginning of a service, led by a 'worship leader', rather than to see the whole service as being an act of worship. It is just as much worship to give in the offering as it is to sing, 'O worship the King, all glorious above'. In church on a Sunday the individual worship we give to God from Monday to Saturday is brought together in a corporate act. That is the prime purpose of the Church – to worship God *collectively*.

Worship relates not only to the songs we sing, the prayers we pray, and the thanks we give, but to everything we do when we gather together as the people of God. A leader who says, 'Let's have a time of worship before we listen to the message,' shows that he or she doesn't understand what true worship involves. Worship should not stop when the sermon starts.

How do you see God?

In Romans 1:18–25, the apostle Paul argues that the essence of sin is a failure to worship the Creator. Our instinct to worship is God-given. We were created to worship. It is possible to observe a faint echo of this design in our instinctive need to applaud great performers or in our adulation of pop stars or sports personalities. Sin, however, perverts this innate desire to worship God and diverts it to lesser objects. 'They neither glorified him as God nor gave thanks to him … and worshipped and served created things rather than the Creator …' (Rom. 1:21,25). The late Francis Schaeffer said, 'The beginning of man's rebellion against God was, and is, the lack of a thankful heart … The rebellion is the deliberate refusal to be the creature before the Creator, to the extent of being thankful.'

We were created to worship.

Paul also talks in this passage about those who 'exchanged the glory of the immortal God for images made to look like mortal man and birds and animals and reptiles' (v.23). We have a name for this type of thing – *idolatry*. Idolatry, however, is not only the worship of false gods; it is also the worship of the true God in a false way. In the words of A.W. Tozer, 'Idolatry is the entertaining of ideas about God that are unworthy of Him.'

How do you see God? What concept of the Almighty do you carry deep down in your heart? What thoughts form in your mind and what feelings are aroused within you when you see that short yet profound three-lettered word *God*? The answers to those questions will determine the depth or shallowness of your worship. You cannot truly worship God if you carry in your heart a wrong or unworthy concept of Him. That is a law that is as fixed as the law of gravity.

Christian idolaters

What comes into our minds when we think about God is most important. Worship is pure or base according to whether the worshipper entertains high or low thoughts about God. A wrong concept of Him can lead to wrong conclusions about Him. For example, if you entertain the thought that God does not have your highest interests at heart then it will most certainly affect the way you worship Him. You cannot worship someone you don't trust.

Each one of us would do well to pause and ask again the questions we posed in the last section: What is my image of God? How do I see Him? What concept of the Creator do I carry in my heart? How, for instance, does the picture the apostle Paul gives of God in Ephesians 1:3–14 compare with your own image of God? Is it similar or radically different? The reason why Paul could speak of God so powerfully was because He saw Him clearly.

Following on from what we have said about idolatry, it is worth noting this statement made by Dr E. Stanley Jones: 'The Church is filled with Christian idolaters, for idolatry consists not only in kneeling before visible objects and giving them obeisance but also of carrying in our hearts a picture of God which is unworthy of Him.' The idolatrous heart assumes that God is other than He is – in itself a monstrous sin – and substitutes for the true God one made after its own likeness. Make sure your concept of God is drawn from Scripture otherwise you may be holding in your mind a false picture of Him.

'Your God is my devil'

On one occasion Martin Luther said to some of his critics, 'Your God is my devil'. That's rather a strange comment to make, you might think, but Luther was taking to task the priests of his day who were opposed to him and saw God as stern, punitive, demanding and angry. They seemed to know nothing of the love that God had for sinners in sending His Son to be their Saviour. In other words, they carried a concept of God that was unworthy of Him. Luther himself viewed God in those harsh terms early in his life. However, one day he received a revelation from Scripture which revolutionised his concept of God, and that revelation led to what we now call the Reformation.

If you could be present in a Christian counselling room when a counsellee is asked 'How do you see God?' you would be astonished at some of the answers that are given. This is how one woman answered that question: 'I see God as cold, distant, unconcerned and

> Wrong thoughts about God affect the way we worship Him.

uncommunicative, always angry with me, pushing me to do this and that for Him, but never coming through for me when I need an urgent answer to prayer.' Would it surprise you to learn that that woman found great difficulties in worship? How can you give yourself to a God in whom you have no confidence? The task, therefore, of the counsellor was to help that woman change her image of God.

We must be careful that we do not entertain in our minds any unworthy thoughts about God – thoughts that discredit Him. Hebrews 11:6 tells us the truth about God: He *does* reward those who earnestly seek Him.

Trust – the basis of worship

The very first mention of the word 'worship' in the Bible occurs in Genesis 22:1–19. Abraham, at God's command, is about to set out to sacrifice his son on an altar on one of the mountains in the region of Moriah. Before he begins the ascent he instructs his servants to stay with the donkey while he and Isaac go up the mountain to erect an altar and offer a sacrifice to God. Notice his words to the servants: 'We will worship and then we will come back to you' (v.5). These words lead us to believe that when Abraham said, '*We* will come back to you,' he fully expected that despite God's earlier command to offer his son Isaac as a sacrifice he would return together with the boy.

What an astonishing faith Abraham had in God. If at this point you had been able to ask Abraham the question 'How do you see God?' what do you think he would have said? Probably something along these lines: 'God is faithful to His promises. He will not go back on His word. He has promised me that my descendants will number a great multitude so if Isaac is to die then I have no doubt God will raise him from the dead. I trust the Almighty no matter what' (see Heb. 11:17–19).

Notice also that Abraham's desire to worship God was not in any way diminished by the fact that God had told him to sacrifice his only son. And why? Because in a heart in which there is a confident trust in God there will always be a readiness to worship – even in the face of massive confusion.

Health for the soul
Now we come to reflect on the second time the word

'worship' is mentioned in Scripture. God tells Moses that the first thing the children of Israel must do when they have been delivered from Egypt is to worship Him (see Exod. 3:1–12). This begs the question 'Why does God want His people to worship Him?' Well, one answer is because worship is the right response to God as He is. When great mountaineers are asked 'Why do you want to climb Everest?' they reply 'Because it is there!' So it is with worshippers. We worship God because He exists and because He is who He is – the great Creator God.

Again we make the point that just as it is natural to feel awed by the sight of a beautiful sunset so it is natural to respond to the Creator's beauty and goodness in spontaneous praise. There is

> 'Worship is inner health made audible.'

something unnatural about a person who is drawn to the ugly and repelled by the beautiful. Perhaps that is why C.S. Lewis, in his book *Reflections on the Psalms*, wrote, 'Worship is inner health made audible.' Those who do not worship God live impoverished lives; their souls are unhealthy because the soul is designed to function best when it is in touch with its Creator – when it reaches out to Him in an attitude of praise and worship. One symptom of spiritual sickness in a Christian is that he or she has no desire to worship. Such Christians have become self-centred rather than God-centred.

Worship, then, is not only the right response to God but is healthy for the soul. We function best when our souls reach out to our Creator in worship and praise. There can be no health in the soul if there is no worship in the soul.

Further Study

Psa. 35:9–10; 35:18; 35:27–28; 103:1–6; Rom. 6:8–14

1. Why does the psalmist praise God with his whole being?
2. Why does Paul exhort us to offer ourselves to God?

Psa. 19:1–6; Isa. 44:1–11; 21–23; Acts 14:8–18; 17:24–31

3. How does the prophet contrast God with idols?
4. How does Paul attempt to correct unworthy concepts of God?

Psa. 105:1–11; Heb. 4:14–16

5. What does the psalmist tell us about God?
6. Why can we approach the throne of grace with confidence?

CHAPTER TWO

HE IS EVERYTHING

Exodus 15:1–8; 24:1–18

'The LORD will reign for ever and ever.'
Exodus 15:18

If you take a concordance you will discover that between Exodus 3:1 and Exodus 10:29 the word 'worship' is mentioned more than ten times. Clearly Moses had grasped the fact that the worship of God by the Israelites was of prime importance. There could be no real health in the nation of Israel without worship.

C.S. Lewis, whose writings are so good on the subject of worship and praise, makes the point that there can be no real life in the soul, no completeness in the personality, if true worship of God is absent. He says that to worship God in spirit and in truth is 'simply to be awake, to have entered the real world'. Failure to worship results in great deprivation. We make the point again: no worship, no spiritual health.

In Egypt the children of Israel were impoverished not only physically but spiritually also by their lack of worship. Now, however, all that is to be changed. They are to learn that the God they may have thought of as 'Something' is now to be 'Everything' to them. *Everything*.

When the great conductor Toscanini had finished conducting a brilliant performance of Beethoven's 5th Symphony the audience leapt to their feet, applauding wildly and shouting their delight. Toscanini waved his arms equally wildly, imploring those who were cheering to stop. As soon as they did he turned to the orchestra and shouted hoarsely, 'You are nothing!' Next he pointed to himself and said, 'I am nothing!' Then he cried,

'Beethoven is everything, everything, everything!' That, in effect, is what we do when we worship God. When we worship we are saying, 'He is everything, everything, everything.'

Celebrating His *victory*

We look now at the very first song recorded in the Bible – Exodus 15:1–18 – a fitting response to the amazing miracle of deliverance from Egyptian tyranny. Having arrived safely on the other side of the Red Sea, Moses leads God's people in an exuberant celebration, and thus the Exodus is commemorated in a magnificent hymn of praise. So the children of Israel praise God not only because He exists but also because of what He has done for them in rescuing them from slavery in Egypt.

The song begins by proclaiming God as *the warrior* (v.3) who has fought for the Israelites against their enemies and overcome them. From this point on in Scripture the marching songs of the children of Israel celebrate *God's* 'military prowess', not theirs. They are the battle hymns not of a republic but of a kingdom, and focus on God's presence as the guarantee of success. It is interesting to note that elsewhere the Exodus is presented as a victory not just over Pharaoh but also over the gods of Egypt (Exod. 12:12). In this sense it was a battle fought and won in the spiritual realm.

In recent years there has been some strange teaching in the Christian Church on the subject of spiritual warfare which advocates attacking Satan with words of praise about God. Nowhere is this method mentioned in Scripture. Praise is not a weapon to be directed at the devil; praise is the lifting of the hearts towards God. The archangel Michael, when disputing with the devil, did not resort to praise. He confronted the devil with these words: 'The Lord rebuke you!' (Jude 9). To celebrate God as Creator and Redeemer with conviction and faith is to proclaim His victory over everything. *His* victory, remember, not ours.

Priming the pump

We can learn a lot about praise and worship by examining the wonderful composition of the spontaneous outburst of praise in Exodus 15, known as the Song of Moses and Miriam, which was sung by the Israelites after their deliverance from Egypt. The song goes on to rejoice not only in God's power but also in His *uniqueness* (v.11): 'Who is like you – majestic in holiness, awesome in glory, working wonders?' The Israelites' praise proclaims the fact that the God who creates and redeems and triumphs is incomparable.

Whenever you are at a loss for some reason to praise God, think of His victory over sin and evil at Calvary and the fact of His uniqueness. There is just no one, on earth or in heaven, who can be compared to Him. If those two great truths do not prime the pump of praise then nothing can. The pattern laid down in the Song of

Moses and Miriam is one that we would do well to study and follow.

We ought always to remember that the reason we have been delivered from sin's bondage is in order to worship God. Sir Herbert Butterfield, the great Cambridge historian, said of the Exodus, 'I know of no other case in history where gratitude was carried so far, no other case where gratitude proved to be such a generative thing … It gave the children of Israel a historical event that they could not get over, could not help remembering and, in the first place, it made them historians – historians in a way that no one had been before.' But Israel's deliverance is as nothing compared to what God has done for us in Christ. If Israel could not get over such a physical deliverance then how can we ever get over such a spiritual deliverance? The answer is that we will never get over it either here or in eternity.

There is just no one, on earth or in heaven, who can be compared to Him.

'You're not home yet!'

Because the God who has redeemed Israel is the Creator of the whole world, this first song sung by the children of Israel also emphasises the universal lordship of the Almighty over every nation. The shock waves created by the Exodus are felt by all the nations affected by this act of God – they tremble with fear at the prospect of the conquest of Canaan (vv.15–16).

The point we have made that the victory was God's, and God's alone, is reinforced here by the statement that it was not God's army that accomplished the Exodus but His strong and mighty arm (v.16). Yet this warrior God is also the God of unfailing love who leads His people home (v.17). Here the song prophetically anticipates the conquest of Canaan and the building of the Temple. And it closes with the triumphant acclamation that the Lord will reign for ever and ever.

Consider this fact also, then, in your private times of worship and praise: God is the God of the whole world and His love will always lead His people home. Of course, for the Israelites 'home' was the land God had promised them. For us 'home' is heaven. C.S. Lewis once wrote, 'Our Father refreshes us on the journey with some pleasant inns but will not encourage us to mistake them for home.'

A missionary tells of returning by ship to his home country. As he watched people disembark and walk into the arms of their loved ones who were expecting them he grew somewhat saddened because he realised that there was no one there to welcome him. Rather petulantly he said to the Lord, 'Why couldn't You arrange for me to have someone to welcome me home?' The Lord whispered, 'You're not home yet.'

Do you want to dance?

The awareness of the great deliverance which the children of Israel had experienced in being rescued from Egypt leads Miriam to take a tambourine and dance, whereupon all the women follow her example and sing and dance before the Lord (Exod. 15:19–21).

At this point in the story those of us who are Westerners tend to explain this conduct as Middle Eastern exuberance. However, if this is our reaction we should pause and ask ourselves: Do we ever get so excited about our deliverance from sin's bondage that we want to dance? 'Dance?' you might exclaim. 'Really dance? I thought it was just our hearts that were to "dance at the sound of His name".' The commentator Walter Brueggemann says about this section of Scripture, 'The news is borne and enacted by the women who dance … towards freedom. For a long time they had not been able to dance – too tired, too fearful, too intimidated. God had acted to save and their dancing was a way of asserting they were daughters of Yahweh's freedom.'

You'll never hear better news than the news of what God has done for you in Christ.

As we discuss the physical expressions of Christian joy it is so easy to feel superior and respond, 'Well, you would never catch me dancing in a Christian meeting.' But, at least, do you not sometimes *feel* like dancing when you reflect on what God has done for you in Christ? The indwelling of the Holy Spirit imparts an awareness within us that all is well with our soul. It makes music inside of us. Exuberance and devotion can go hand in hand. Church history bears witness to that. People, even staid and phlegmatic people, often dance or jump with joy when they hear some sensationally good news. Well, you'll never hear better news than the news of what God has done for you in Christ.

Four aspects of worship

From the episode in Exodus 24:1–18 we can discover at least four basic aspects of worship. First, it is important to note that God convenes the meeting. It is the Almighty who invites His people to gather to meet Him as the assembly of the Lord. When Moses gives God's directions, the people respond with one voice and agree to do things God's way (v.3). This suggests to us that worship is God's summons to us and is to be conducted on His terms. In other words, worship is dictated by God's terms, not by our temperament.

Second, the story tells us that in worship different people have different parts to play. Participation is the keynote. Third, the meeting involved listening to God's Word. Without this, worship is incomplete (vv.3,7). No worship service is worthy of the name if it does not strengthen our obedience to God's Word. Fourth, in worship the community is engaged in the renewal of the covenant, so the 'covenant book' is read (in our case, the Bible) and the 'covenant blood' is poured out (for us, the cup of communion). Our relationship with God is sealed and our worship made valid by blood sacrifice (vv.6,8).

Of course, much has changed because of the sacrifice of Jesus – not least that every worshipper can come near to a holy God and has no need to worship at a distance (see v.2). But the other features we have noted are still valid. So remember this: in corporate worship we are summoned by God, everyone has a part to play, and the Word of God must be prominent – and all this because of the shed blood of Jesus.

Further Study
Deut. 10:12–22; Matt. 22:34–40; Rom. 11:33–36
1. What did God ask of Israel?
2. How does Paul indicate that worship is of prime importance?

Psa. 77:10–20; 1 Cor. 15:54–58
3. How does the psalmist celebrate God's uniqueness?
4. What deliverance does Paul celebrate?

Psa. 150:1–6; Luke 15:25–32
5. How exuberant is the psalmist's praise?
6. What does the father celebrate with music and dancing?

CHAPTER THREE

ENJOY!

1 Chronicles 16:7–36
2 Chronicles 20:1–29

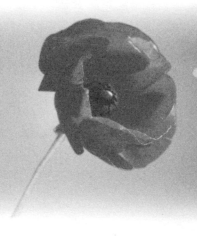

*'Glory in his holy name; let the hearts of those
who seek the LORD rejoice.'*
1 Chronicles 16:10

For a moment now we dip into the book of Deuteronomy, and we see in chapter 12:1–14 that the children of Israel are commanded when they enter the promised land not to worship the Lord their God in the way that heathen people worship their gods. They are to have one central place of worship, and when that place is revealed to them they are to worship *and* rejoice. The Lord encourages them not to enter into worship simply as a duty but as a delight. Worship that has no delight in it is not true worship.

John Piper, an American pastor, frequently makes reference in his writings to the fact that although we do not worship God in order to experience joy, the inevitable consequence of worship is finding deep joy and satisfaction for our souls, including emotional release and wholeness. Piper says, 'Where feelings for God are dead, worship is dead.' Some Christians teach that worship is

> The Lord encourages them not to enter into worship simply as a duty but as a delight.

giving to God and that we ought not to indulge ourselves in the good feelings that the Spirit stirs within us as a result. This is nonsense of course. Although it is wrong to worship God in order to experience joy, there is nothing wrong with enjoying the feelings that flow into our hearts as a consequence of worship.

Theologians throughout the ages have said that our destiny is not only to work for God but to enjoy Him also. The more you give your mind and thoughts to Him the more joy will fill your heart. Don't deny those feelings or attempt to smother them. They are the inevitable result of worship. So enjoy!

Songs we still sing

The incident in 1 Chronicles 15:1–24 throws a further beam of light on this intriguing subject of worship. David's actions seem astonishingly bold. He leaves the tabernacle of Moses, with its animal sacrifices and priesthood, at Gibeon, and erects another tent in Jerusalem. There, once the dedicatory offering had been made, only the non-sacrificial worship of praise and prayer operated. This was an amazing innovation which lasted 40 years until Solomon built the Temple and fused Davidic praise with Mosaic ritual.

Often David's action is seen as a prophetic one pointing to that praise which lies beyond animal sacrifices in the kingdom of God. From this time on the worship in David's tabernacle provided the pattern for the conduct of worship in Israel. It was David's tabernacle, we should note, that gave birth to the psalms (cf 1 Chron. 16:7–36). David's arrangements for the establishment of praise in the new tabernacle in Jerusalem make for challenging reading. Worship was not a disorderly free-for-all. It was led by those who had consecrated themselves to this sacred task (v.12), and were committed to God's way of doing things (v.13). Musical skill and training were encouraged and were not seen as a denial of spirituality (v.22). The priority was joyful singing to balanced musical accompaniment (v.16) – not, as is so often the case in today's Church, feeble singing drowned out by overamplified music!

So rich and true was this worship introduced in Old Testament times that its songs, if not its tunes, have lasted for 3,000 years. The truths expressed in the psalms of David are with us today. We sing them still!

'No flags at half mast'

When David established the new form of worship in Jerusalem he wanted everything to be done in a considered and thoughtful, as well as a joyful, way. But he knew that what mattered above all was the presence of God in worship, and this was symbolised by the ark of the covenant. Nothing else really mattered. The ark was the wooden box covered with gold which had once stood in the Most Holy Place in the tabernacle. It was the visual symbol of God's presence, and regarded as the earthly footstool of His heavenly throne.

David knew the ark had been neglected in Saul's reign (1 Chron. 13:3) and was determined to restore it to its central place in worship. The king was so exuberant about this that he stripped off his royal outer garments and, clothed in a linen undergarment like a priest, led the procession into the city in an unselfconscious dance of joy. Not for the last time did someone find such exuberance offensive and unbecoming. David's response to his critical wife is that he will become even more undignified than this if it means celebrating the Lord's presence with His people (cf. 2 Sam. 6:21–22).

As we said before, people express themselves in different ways in worship – for instance, some dance and others do not. But the great C.H. Spurgeon's advice surely applies to us all: 'Never hang your flag at half mast when you praise God! No, run up every colour, let every banner wave in the breeze, and let all the powers and passions of your spirit exult and rejoice in God your Saviour.' Surely even the most restrained among us owe God that! If worship doesn't get to your feet then at least let it get to your heart. Remember: no flags at half mast!

The 'Amen mentality'

Worship in Old Testament times was most certainly a multimedia event! No one, we imagine, ever fell asleep in David's tabernacle – at least not while the songs rang out, cymbals clashed, trumpets sounded, and the harps and lyres were strummed. But everything was done with a clear purpose.

As we see from verse 4 of 1 Chronicles 16, the priestly leaders were appointed to do three things: first, to make petitions to the Lord; second, to thank God by publicly acknowledging what He had done; third, to praise God and extol His name. The musicianship of gifted people supported the offering of praise. It was in this atmosphere that some of the best-known psalms originated – as the two examples given in this chapter indicate. We will look at these in more detail later.

Notice also that when the psalms had been sung all the people said 'Amen' and 'Praise the LORD'. How important it is in corporate worship to cultivate this 'Amen mentality'. Not every worshipper takes part in everything at every moment, but everyone is expected to participate by being attentive and worshipful and by being willing to give ready assent to all that is offered. Corporate worship is not the sum total of many individuals 'doing their own thing', as we say, but involves all of us affirming the faith we share as the people of God in joyful and wholehearted agreement.

Sunday worship would be revolutionised if there were more response from the congregation, especially in those churches which do not use a liturgy. How rich and heart-warming it is when the people of God give a hearty 'Amen' to the truths enunciated in His presence.

Worth singing about
As we have noted, the major innovations David made in

the new tabernacle in Jerusalem gave rise to some of the collections of psalms. The ancient historian shows us this by inserting in his narrative in 1 Chronicles 16 two typical psalms – Psalm 105:1–15 and Psalm 96.

The first song, for which Asaph is the spokesman, celebrates the unique identity of Israel among the nations. The psalmist sings first of God's *miraculous power* which redeemed Israel from slavery and created a people to glorify His name (vv.8–13). God's people owe everything to God – to the wonders He has performed on their behalf. 'Let the hearts of those who seek the Lord rejoice' in this!

> God's people have good reason to praise Him when they consider His ability and eagerness to keep His promises.

The song also heralds the *marvellous promises* of God (vv.15–18). God's people have good reason to praise Him when they consider His ability and eagerness to keep His promises. In this particular instance God is praised for the redemptive promises He kept which He had made with Abraham centuries before. Keep this fact always in mind: we worship a covenant-making and covenant-keeping God. We can so easily forget our promises but He never forgets the ones He has made.

Lastly, the prophetic singer rejoices in the *miraculous protection* God has afforded the Israelites (vv.19–22).

Throughout their history God had protected and preserved them and thus shown that they were His anointed ones – His chosen people. The Israelites had something to make a song and dance about. So also do we. This soul-redeeming, promise-keeping, protecting God of the Old Testament is our God also. What He is He was, and what He was He is, and what He was and is He ever will be. Amen.

Bowing before beauty

The second sample psalm (1 Chron. 16:23–36), can be found also as Psalm 96. How wonderfully it illustrates the extraordinary range of worship in the Bible. What God has done for His people demands the attention of all the earth (v.24). The first psalm (vv.7–22) had celebrated the *mystery* of Israel – a special nation whose existence can only be explained by supernatural power and promises and protection. The song we are looking at now heralds the *message* which Israel has to tell to the nations. The very existence of the Israelites as a worshipping people demonstrates the unique and timeless glory of God. To declare this God as the one true God is to dethrone all the idols of the other nations (vv.25–26).

Israel also exists to declare God's *present rule*. All the families and nations in the world – indeed, the joy-filled heavens and trembling earth – are recruited to share the happy conviction that 'the LORD reigns' (v.33). Notice the invitation in verse 29.

In the parallel verse (Psa. 96:9) Eugene Peterson paraphrases this as 'Bow before the beauty of God' (*The Message*). When God's people enter into worship there is a sense in which their hearts succumb to His overwhelming attractiveness. As we said earlier, the more we know of God the more attractive He becomes to our souls. Finally, the song turns our eyes and hopes towards God's *future coming* (v.33). Even while we rejoice in God's present kingship we relish the prospect that one day He will come to fully establish His kingdom of justice.

These three dimensions of God's Person and work fuel our thanksgiving and praise (vv.34–36) and evoke a hearty 'Amen'. Should we not echo that 'Amen'?

Prophetic praising

Buried deep in the historical books of the Old Testament are thoughts and ideas that are worth more than gold when it comes to understanding biblical worship. In the first eight verses of 1 Chronicles 25, with an historian's eye for detail, the chronicler records how David had arranged for worship to be conducted. Once more we observe that there is nothing haphazard about the arrangements. Though there is room, as we shall see, for spontaneity, most of the activity related to worship was thought through. This did not make it unspiritual. Quite the contrary.

What is especially illuminating about this passage is that

it shows that praising God is essentially a prophetic activity. To prophesy in the Old Testament is nearly always to speak forth God's word. There is foretelling, of course, but, even more important, there is forthtelling – speaking out God's message both in word and in song. Do you realise, therefore, that when you sing out your praises to God you are acting prophetically?

Remember this also: when we worship we are doing much more than merely expressing a passing mood. In singing songs which have a credal and gospel content we are prophetically declaring the truth of what God has done and said. We are prophetically proclaiming how great and good and gracious God is and what He has achieved. What is more, through praise we prophetically celebrate not only what God is doing among us now but what He plans to do in the future too. We sing of His past salvation, His present rule, and His coming kingdom. And because our praise is truly prophetic we help to bring about what God has promised and planned. This is why nothing must ever take the place of worship in the Christian Church. Nothing.

Spiritual warfare

The story in 2 Chronicles 20:1–29 of how Jehoshaphat defeated Moab and Ammon teaches us some more important lessons about praise and worship. Prepared by prayer and fasting, and emboldened by God's promise that the battle is *His* and not theirs,

Jehoshaphat, king of Judah, sends out singers as his front-line troops.

But look at what they sing. They do not sing these songs *at* the enemy – a point we made earlier – as if praise were a spiritual weapon. These songs are not targeted at the opposition but offered to God in worship. The songs they sing are not martial songs calling down defeat on the enemy. On this occasion they do not even sing of the Lord's power or might. No, they sing boldly of the unfailing *love* of God – that covenant love with which God is committed to His people.

Praise is faith set to music.

Praise is faith set to music. It expresses our confidence in a God who has already won the decisive battles. The way to face the devil when you feel you are a victim of his attacks is not to lash back at him, albeit in God's name, with angry denunciations. Simply declare boldly that the Lord loves you, keeps His covenant with you, and will never forsake you. The fight we have in nearly every case of fear and danger is the fight of faith – or indeed, *for* faith. It is the struggle to maintain our confidence in the Lord at all costs. Nothing strengthens faith more in such circumstances than to join in the chorus of defiant praise: 'God is indeed good, and His covenant love lasts for ever.' But remember: by praising we do not so much fight the battle as proclaim the victory of our God. This more than any other one thing is the secret of spiritual warfare.

Further Study

2 Chron. 30:1–5; 30:13–16; 30:21–27; Luke 10:21–24

1. How was Israel's worship both a duty and a delight?
2. Why did Jesus rejoice?

Psa. 118:1–4; 15–24; Acts 3:1–10

3. What good reasons does the psalmist give for thanksgiving?
4. Why does the crippled beggar make such a 'song and dance'?

Exod. 14:13–18; Psa. 136:1–4; 16–26; Phil. 2:6–11

5. How did the Israelites set their history in God to music?
6. How did Paul celebrate the story of Jesus?

CHAPTER FOUR

REAL WORSHIP
FOR A REAL GOD

Job 1:6–22
Psalm 89:46–52
Psalm 22:1–11

'Ascribe to the LORD the glory due to his name …'
Psalm 29:2

The revival that took place under Hezekiah, described in 2 Chronicles 29, saw the restoration of all that was best about worship in the Old Testament. It reinstated many of the features of Israel's worship which we have already mentioned.

Not surprisingly, the worship had to be re-established in the way prescribed by David (v.25), and under prophetic direction. Clearly, it was also a priestly activity which was led by the Levites (v.26) who were consecrated (v.34). Sacrifice was at the heart of it too (vv.27–35). The shedding of blood at the Passover, which marked the nation's original deliverance, was continued in the regular animal sacrifices at the tabernacle and then at the Temple. Later we will note how this was both reaffirmed and radically redefined by the once-for-all sacrifice of Jesus on the cross.

Consider now the fact that in the revival of true worship under Hezekiah singing was a prominent feature (vv.27–30). The songs sung were those composed by or dedicated to David and so almost certainly included some of the psalms that we know (v.30). The music was lively and varied, although we can only imagine how it sounded! The praise was lyrical and expressed gladness (v.30). It was vocal and it was physical, involving kneeling and bowing the head. The worship scene we see in 2 Chronicles 29:1–36 was one that impacted all the senses, affected the whole personality, and involved the whole assembly (v.28).

Surely the worship of God enacted at the time of the revival under Hezekiah represents the high-water mark of Old Testament worship. Should not Christian worship at least be equal to it if not exceed it?

The highest form of worship

As we journey through the Old Testament we come to what is considered one of the oldest books in the Bible – Job. What a picture the opening words of this book give us of a man's determination to worship God no matter what his circumstances.

Satan, we are told, came before God and said, 'Does Job fear God for nothing? … stretch out your hand and strike everything he has, and he will surely curse you to your face' (Job 1:9,11). Satan is given permission to interfere in Job's life, and one day, like a bolt out of the blue, tidings of disaster shook him to the core. Hot on the heels of one another come the messengers of woe. The reports are desolating. His oxen and donkeys have gone, his sheep and camels have gone, his servants have gone, and then his children have gone. With a single stroke he has lost almost everything. But think of the moral splendour of this: Job, hearing the numbing news, falls on the ground and *worships* (Job 1:20–21).

How many of us, in similar circumstances, would

have responded in this way? Clearly Job possessed the conviction that God was to be worshipped not only because of what He does but for who He is. As we have already seen, one part of worship involves giving God praise for what He has done for us, but the highest form of worship is worship that is given to God just for who He is. It is easy to worship God when everything goes right; it is not so easy, however, when everything goes wrong. It all goes back to what we were saying earlier about the issue of trust. Job trusted God and believed that He had good reasons for allowing what had happened. And we say again: that kind of trust means we offer the highest form of worship.

Justifying God's goodness
We move now into the book of Psalms. This book, more than any other book in the Bible, takes us to the depths of worship and praise and was, as you know, the hymnbook of the ancient Israelites.

The song which we will look at, Psalm 22, gives the lie to the suggestion (as we saw with Job) that worship is possible only when things are going right. Far from it. Worship is not a superficial response to the blue skies and fairness of life. The Bible's richest worship is a cry of praise from the depths and from the darkness. It is the God-forsaken, it is interesting to note, who affirm that God is 'enthroned' on the 'praise' of His people (v.3).

How can we continue to celebrate our trust in a God

who is always right in a world where often so much is wrong? Worship in times of darkness is the defiant answer of faith to praise God if not *for* everything then certainly *in* everything. As the great theologian G.C. Berkouwer memorably said, 'The remarkable fact is that all the questions that arise in Scripture around what we call the problem of theodicy [a term used for arguments which justify God's goodness in a world where evil exists] have their profoundest and most definitive answer in a "hallelujah!"' He went on, 'The wonder is that the paeans of praise arise so often in hard times, that the songs are heard so frequently from the shadow, and that the doxology is sung as the last candle-light of life's joy flickers.'

> Worship in times of darkness is the defiant answer of faith to praise God if not *for* everything then certainly *in* everything.

How glorified the Lord is when we refuse to allow the God-denying look of things to hinder us from giving Him worship and praise.

We know His name

In Psalm 29 the psalmist draws our attention to another reason why we should ascribe glory to God: because of His *name*.

Christians are not like the Athenians who erected an

altar 'to the *unknown* god' (Acts 17:23). We know God's *name*. As you are aware, a relationship is transformed when we are able to call a person by their name. God has revealed Himself to us as a *personal* God who can be known personally and loved and worshipped. Our praise, therefore, is not something that is unfocused – a shot in the dark; it centres on His name. One of the key acclamations of the Bible is 'Hallelujah' (translated in our Bibles as 'Praise the LORD', eg Psa. 106:1,48). The word is made up of two parts: 'hallel' (to praise) and 'yah' or 'yahweh' which is God's covenant name, made known to Moses at the burning bush when He declared 'I AM WHO I AM' (Exod. 3:14). Jesus took that great mysterious name of God and linked it to simple things that we can understand when He said, 'I am the gate' (John 10:7), 'I am the light' (John 8:12), 'I am the good shepherd' (John 10:11), 'I am the way and the truth and the life' (John 14:6).

Biblical worship is many things, one of them being a joyous celebration of the fact that God has revealed to us His name – a name that spells out reliability, faithfulness, love, mercy, deliverance, power and compassion. How wonderful. How truly wonderful.

The most important thing

In Psalm 29 we are urged to *glorify* the Lord and exalt His name together. Glorifying God should be our number one priority when we gather together to worship the Lord.

The theologian Donald McCullough says, 'What we do on Sunday mornings ... the order of events and the manner in which we enact the drama ... must always point to God, must reinforce again and again that God has taken the initiative and called us together, that God's grace is more important than our sin, that God's will is more important than our desires, and that God's glorification is more important than our edification.' We should not take that last sentence to mean that our edification is unimportant; what he is saying is that God's glorification is *more* important.

Glorifying God should be our number one priority when we gather together to worship the Lord.

To lose sight of that is to lose sight of the true purpose of the Church. Those responsible for leading a Christian service ought always to have a keen eye for ensuring that God's name is glorified in every single thing that is done.

A song that has been introduced into the Christian Church relatively recently contains a thought that should always be present in our hearts when we come together, even though we may not actually sing the words:

I'm coming back to the heart of worship ...
It's all about You, Jesus ...

It's not about me …
It's all about You.
                    Matt Redman

Perhaps if we were more anxious to glorify the name of Jesus than the name of our church, pastor or denomination then our services might throb more with the energy of the Spirit than they do at present.

Thank You

One of the key elements of worship, we said earlier, is the giving of thanks. The psalm we turn to now, Psalm 35, begins with a prayer for divine protection but then includes the psalmist's pledge to give God thanks for the deliverance he is sure He will grant him.

Biblical scholar, Ronald Allen, points out that the Hebrew language has no word that can be used to simply say 'thank you'. In Old Testament times you expressed your thanks by telling other people how good a particular person had been to you. What is more, it was customary to praise people not to their face but in front of others – to 'sing their praises', as we say. Similarly, praise of God was a *public* declaration in which He was acclaimed for His mercy and love. Worship in Old Testament times was therefore a form of witness because congregational praise of God's greatness and grace spilled over into public testimony to Him before the listening world. In this way the wider audience was invited to join the chorus of praise raised by the family of faith.

The pastor of a large and constantly growing church in the Far East begins every service by encouraging all those present – Christians and those not yet Christians – to give thanks to God. He says something like this: 'Think about God's goodness to you over the past week. He has given you air to breathe, water to drink, food to eat, and so many other things. Join with us now in thanking and praising Him for His goodness.' Touched by reminders of God's goodness, hundreds are ready to repent before the service really starts. It gives new meaning to the words, 'the goodness of God leads you to repentance' (Rom. 2:4, NKJV).

'Praise in a minor key'

We cannot discuss the subject of worship without touching on the issue of lament. 'Lament', according to the dictionary, is 'a passionate expression of grief'. But, you might ask, what has lament to do with worship and praise? Old Testament theologian Bernhard Anderson says that lament is *praise offered in a minor key*.

When did you last hear a lament in your church? Psalm 80 can be described as a 'community lament' – a cry of anguish from God's people because they are grieved by their own failure and God's seeming absence. Three out of ten psalms are laments and so, as someone has remarked, they 'far outnumber any other kind of songs in the Psalter' – a fact that is not well reflected in our contemporary songbooks! The upsurge of praise is a necessary part of worship but too often it is at the expense of the admission of our failures and the facing of reality. In some churches which do not use a liturgy, supplication and petition have been all but swept aside by a tide of rejoicing, while penitential songs have sunk without trace beneath a flood of overconfident celebration. Community lament lies at the heart of intercession and of our plea for revival. And we need to learn once again how to pray like this: 'Restore us, O God; make your face shine upon us, that we may be saved' (vv.3,7).

God is not easily offended and can bear our anguished questions of 'How long?' and 'Why?' (vv.4,12). The freedom to complain to God is a feature of Israel's relationship with Him. Without it worship is untruthful. Lament should be understood as complaining with confidence – admitting to God how we really feel because we are confident He will hear our prayer.

On being real

The book of Psalms, as we pointed out earlier, was the hymnbook of the people of God. The psalms were sung publicly in the same way that we sing our modern hymns. But what do you think would happen if Psalm 88 were set to music and sung in your church next Sunday?

Can you imagine people singing, 'But I cry to you for help, O LORD ... Why, O LORD, do you reject me and hide your face from me' (vv.13–14)? Be honest, though. Aren't there times when you feel like that? Most Christians respond to their negative feelings by pretending they do not exist. By doing so they think they are being spiritual, but actually they are ducking into denial. Integrity involves facing whatever is true.

Integrity involves facing whatever is true.

Earlier we made the comment that lament is 'praise offered in a minor key'. Many Christians do not much like the minor key. They prefer their songs to be upbeat and joyful. Walter Brueggemann says, 'There is an enormous temptation for "high faith" to deny the dark side of life when things do not work ... against that common failure the psalms of lament make contact with the emotions of failure.' We seem to be as afraid of lament as we do of catching a serious case of the flu. Why is this? Is it because we fail to see that openness and honesty is the soil out of which grow true confidence and joy?

The ancient Israelites sang their songs of lament as worshipfully as they sang their hymns of praise. They were able to express their emotional struggles as part of their worship, knowing that God would not turn His face away from them. God delights in our passionate engagement with Him, and what He longs for is that all His children be real.

When God becomes real

Though denial causes us to gloss over negative feelings that occasionally arise within us, the verses in the psalms expressing lament help us to acknowledge them. John Calvin, the sixteenth-century Reformer, said, 'The psalmists lay open their inmost thoughts and affections and call, or rather draw, each one of us to the examination of himself in particular in order that none of the infirmities to which we are subject and of the many vices in which we may abound may remain concealed.'

The writer of Psalm 89 cries, 'How long, O LORD? Will you hide yourself for ever?' (v.46). Don't you feel as you read those words that the psalmist is battling with some deep-seated emotions? He is being ruthlessly honest, however, as he seeks to be as real as it is possible to be. We don't know for sure but it is possible that the psalmist's natural instinct was to pretend that he was not feeling the way he was. Whether or not that was the case, honesty and integrity caused him to look into the depth of his soul and admit to his true feelings.

We need never be afraid of expressing our real feelings in God's presence. The following may be worded rather clumsily but we hope you get the point nevertheless: the more real we are with God the more real we will discover Him to be.

Further Study

Psa. 4:1–8; Hab. 3:1–4; 17–19

1. How does the psalmist express his trust in God?
2. In what circumstances will the prophet still rejoice?

Jonah 2:1–9; Acts 16:25–34

3. What impresses you about Jonah's prayer?
4. How did Paul and Silas express defiant faith and what resulted?

Psa. 142:1–7; Mark 14:32–41

5. Reflect on the psalmist's honesty before God.
6. Ponder the reality of Jesus' experience in Gethsemane.

CHAPTER FIVE

OPEN THE DOOR

Psalm 103:1–22
Isaiah 6:1–13
Hosea 2:8–15

'Praise the LORD, O my soul;
all my inmost being, praise his holy name.'
Psalm 103:1

It may be that the chapters up until now which have stressed the importance of worship have made some of you who are struggling with serious and pressing problems feel a little threatened. Perhaps you are saying to yourself, 'When I go to church my problems seem to overwhelm all other thoughts and make it difficult for me to concentrate on giving God praise. If the truth be known, I am more interested in finding solutions to my problems than focusing on praise.' If that is the way you feel and you are willing to admit it then full marks for honesty!

A song sung in some sections of the Church has a line which goes like this: 'Let's forget about ourselves and concentrate on Him and worship Him.' This is easier said than done when life is filled with problems. But though it is not an easy thing to do, it is not impossible. In Psalm 103 the psalmist seems to be holding a conversation with his soul. He talks to his soul and says in effect, 'Come on, soul. Do what you are supposed to do and begin to praise the Lord.' Although it is true, as we have been saying, that worship and praise is our response to God, there are times when our soul is in a state of spiritual idleness and so we need to take the initiative and begin to praise Him – even though we may not feel like it.

God has made you as a choosing being, so the next time

God has made you as a choosing being.

you don't feel like worshipping choose to do so anyway. You may find, as thousands before you have found, that the door you open to God in your soul is the door through which He comes to renew you and refresh you.

'The feel-God factor'

True worship connects us with reality – the ultimate reality of God's supreme sovereignty. When we worship we approach the throne occupied by the One who made and controls the universe. This is why worship can be a world-shattering, world-changing event. When we worship we are symbolically and spiritually reordering our disordered lives around God, recentring them on His true authority.

Isaiah, in Isaiah 6:1–13, is given a vision of heaven's worship, as was the apostle John, centuries later on the island of Patmos. His experience reminds us further of the crucial fact that whenever we gather to worship we are joining a worship meeting that is already in progress! We meet Sunday by Sunday not only with our fellow worshippers but also with angels and archangels and the whole company of heaven. Such exalted worship enlarges the scale of our lives and opens a space for God to fill, and thus the consequence of our worship is that heaven's will is done on earth. Like Isaiah, we may discover that an encounter with the awesome holiness of God is as powerful as a huge electric shock is to the physical system! And our unclean lips – soiled by profaning God's name – are cleansed and purged.

The most wonderful thing about worship, as Isaiah realised, is that through it we are connected to the heartfelt concerns of God. Far too often we go to church hoping that our own concerns will be addressed. True worship has more to do with a 'feel-God' factor than a 'feel-good' factor. And here's the remarkable thing: the more we enter into the concerns of God the less significant our own concerns become.

> The more we enter into the concerns of God the less significant our own concerns become.

'To enjoy Him for ever'

Early on in this book we asked the question 'Why should we worship?' One answer, we said, is that we worship because of who God is. A further answer is this: *because we were created to worship*. The shorter version of the famous *Westminster Catechism* asks the question 'What is the chief end of man?' and answers it this way: 'The chief end [purpose or aim] of man is to glorify God and to enjoy Him for ever.' God's ultimate purpose in creating us was so that we could worship and praise Him. Isaiah, in the passage before us, confirms the fact that God formed His people that they might proclaim His praise (43:14–21).

David, you might remember, asked 'Will the dust praise you?' (Psa. 30:9), in other words, 'Shall the dead praise You?', as if God cannot afford to let anyone die. But whereas the psalmist makes the need to praise God a reason for staying alive, we ought not to forget in passing that it is one reason God has appointed us to spend eternity with Him. In the words of the hymn writer, 'Our days of praise shall never be past, while life and thought and being last, and immortality endures.'

In our giving, God gives Himself to us.

To return to the point we made earlier, the less self-absorbed we are, and the more we worship, the more we become the people we are meant to be. Though we should not worship for the effect it has upon us, nevertheless worship does have a profound effect upon us. William Temple put it like this: 'To worship is to quicken the conscience by the holiness of God, to feed the mind with the truth of God, to purge the imagination by the beauty of God, to open the heart to the love of God, and to devote the will to the purpose of God.' We give our worship to God and, in our giving, God gives Himself to us. And how!

Holy reality

Often the Old Testament prophets come across as being very serious and severe and sometimes what they say doesn't make for pleasant reading. That is one reason why a number of Christians steer clear of the Old Testament. But Christians are supposed to live in two Testaments – the Old as well as the New. In the interests of truth we must look, therefore, at a prophetic exposure of false worship.

In Jeremiah 7:1–15 we see Jeremiah at the very gate of the Temple denouncing the inconsistency between the people's way of life and their way of worship. The prophet's sermon attacks the practice of worshipping in the Temple while outside its confines the poor are being ill-treated (v.6). Dietrich Bonhoeffer, the Lutheran pastor murdered by the Nazis, famously challenged the Church in Germany, which at that time was blind to the persecution of the Jews, with these words: 'Only those who cry out for the Jews have the right to sing Gregorian chants.' There were those in the Temple at Jerusalem – especially the ruling élite – who no doubt thought Jerusalem was inviolable, and that God would protect His people no matter how cynical and corrupt they became. They needed to be reminded of the truth that 'judgment begins with the family of God' (see 1 Pet. 4:17). Though the worship centre at Shiloh had once been a dwelling-place for God's name, God had destroyed it, and Jerusalem would suffer the same fate (v.12). 'The Temple,' says Walter Brueggemann, 'had become a means of cover-up for the destructive way life is lived in the real world.'

True worship is a meeting with holy reality. Our lives

are only as good as our worship, and our worship is only as good as our lives.

First things first

We look now at another Old Testament prophet who emphasises the point just made, namely that acceptable worship is inseparable from acceptable living. Hosea condemns the way Israel had adopted the culture of Canaan and, in particular, was assimilating the worship of the local pagan god, Baal.

'Baalism' was tailored to the human desire for health, wealth and prosperity. In fact, Baal was a prosperity god whose worship was meant to guarantee fertility and success. The worship of Baal was highly sensual and even included prostitution. It was designed to arouse religious feelings. Commenting on some Western worship Eugene Peterson says, 'The phrase "Let's have a worship experience" is really Baalism's substitute for "Let us worship God"'. Prostitution, or harlotry, took place in a physical sense but also became a metaphor for spiritual fornication, that is, worship equated with 'whoreship'. To quote Peterson again: 'Baal worship sought fulfilment through self-expression, worship that accepted the needs and passions of the worshipper as raw material. "Harlotry" is worship which says: "I will give you satisfaction. You want religious feelings? I will give them to you. You want your needs fulfilled? I'll do it in the form most attractive to you."'

We must be careful that we do not import into our worship the attitudes of the culture of our day. The spirit of the age leads us to crave excitement and seek sensations. In this 'therapeutic culture', as it has been called, people want to be either entertained or soothed and stroked and made to feel better about themselves. Is that what we seek when we gather to worship together? God help us if it be so.

Half-baked Christians

The way in which a wrong concept of God destroys a person's spiritual life is seen most dramatically in the life of Ephraim – one of the tribes of Israel. There was a time when God was the sole object of the worship of those belonging to this tribe. Hosea tells us in, 'When Ephraim spoke, men trembled; he was exalted in Israel. But he became guilty of Baal worship and died' (Hosea 13:1). Hosea is referring here to the fact that in the beginning Ephraim was a powerful tribe from which came the great leader Joshua. Now, however, Ephraim is charged with having turned from serving the true God and bowing the knee to an idol – Baal.

You can be sure that didn't happen all at once. The change would have come gradually. Perhaps the people became more interested in men's opinion than in God's. Or perhaps pride took over and they started to usurp God's position. One thing is sure: the moment they allowed the picture of God to be changed in their minds their life started to disintegrate. Listen to this: 'When Ephraim saw his sickness … [he] turned to Assyria' (Hosea 5:13). Their own power gone, they align themselves with the strongest power of the day.

Keep close to the picture of God presented in the Scriptures.

Ephraim is a type of those half-baked Christians who have a part of their lives turned towards God and a part to the world. In such people decay quickly sets in. One of the most important things we can do to maintain a strong spiritual life is to ensure that we keep close to the picture of God presented in the Scriptures. Once we allow ourselves to 'make God in our own image' our lives quickly start to fall apart. We urge you to stay close to Scripture. Study it regularly. It will teach you all you need to know about God and how He is to be worshipped.

When God doesn't show up

As we go through these issues we must keep in mind the thought that we are using the word 'worship' in its broadest sense to cover the whole of life's response to God. If nothing else, this sharply reminds us that we cannot sincerely join in the public praise of God if our daily lives are being lived in direct contradiction of His commandments.

In Amos 5:21–27 we find that though the worship

services are crowded, the singing enthusiastic, and the offerings lavish, the worshippers' daily lives are corrupt and ungodly and they are oppressing the poor and needy. Amos bravely exposes the form of worship that was masking unethical behaviour. God will not tolerate such hypocrisy, he says. When people meet in God's name to worship Him in a phoney way one thing is sure: God doesn't turn up! As Alec Motyer puts it, 'Their worship was dutiful, exceedingly costly – think of the outlay on animals for sacrifice – apparently whole-hearted, emotionally satisfying, but if religion does not get through to God it has failed centrally.'

One of the worship centres used by the Israelites was at Gilgal (Amos 4:4). Ironically, Gilgal had gained its name from the time when God had rolled away their reproach (Josh. 5:9). Now the people were not 'holy-rollers' but '*unholy*-rollers'! If there's any 'rolling' to be done now, says Amos, let it be the 'rolling down' of the river of God's pure justice to clean up society (Amos 5:24). True worship depends not on how loudly we sing or on the musical competence of the worship team. Rather, it depends on how clean our hearts are. Chris Wright's words bear repeating: 'Acceptable worship is inseparable from acceptable living.'

Further Study

Psa. 99:1–9; Luke 2:8–20; Heb. 12:28–29; 13:22–24

1. Celebrate with the psalmist a God who is holy.
2. Reflect on the reactions of the shepherds.

Psa. 8:1–9; 139:1–7; 13–16; 23–24; Matt. 21:9–16

3. How does God touch the deepest springs of our being?
4. What praise does Jesus accept?

Exod. 31:18–32:8; Hosea 8:1–12; 1 John 5:21; Jude 1–5, 17–25

5. What happened when Israel turned away from God's Word?
6. How does Jude encourage his readers to stay true to revealed truth?

CHAPTER SIX

'IN SPIRIT AND IN TRUTH'

Luke 10:38–42
John 4:1–26
1 Corinthians 11:17–34

*'Yet a time is coming and has now come
when the true worshippers will worship
the Father in spirit and in truth ...'*
John 4:23

It is time now to start exploring the New Testament to discover some of the things it has to tell us about worship. In Matthew 2:1–12 we come across the very first reference to the word 'worship' in the New Testament Scriptures. We read that Magi, or Wise Men, from the east, having seen a strange star in the heavens and having recognised it as a sign that the Son of God had come to earth, travelled to Jerusalem to worship Him.

It's rather strange that though the ancient seers of Israel had strained their eyes in the darkness and caught a glimpse of the fact one day God's Son would visit this earth, the first to tell of the fulfilment of those prophecies were not Jews but Gentiles. As one Bible commentator says, 'This time Magi forestalled Israel who possessed the clear prophetic word.' We can only speculate as to what went on in the minds of the Magi as they looked down on the Christ child. Did they realise that the baby lying there before them would change the nature of worship for ever?

The Jews affirmed their belief in one living God. 'Hear, O Israel,' they said over and over again, 'the Lord is one.' By implication this meant that all other 'gods' were imaginary deities. The birth of Jesus revealed that there is a second Person in what we now call the 'Trinity' – someone who is equal to God, who, like Him, is eternal, and who has been with Him from the beginning. There was a time when Jesus

'True God of true God.'

became man, but never a time when He became God. He was man from the manger but God from all eternity. And when we bow before Him and worship Him we are worshipping One who is God. In the words of the Nicene Creed, 'true God of true God'.

The urgent and the important

We touch now on the story of Mary and Martha in Luke 10:38–42 – a story that underlines the fact that though we can worship God through our work, we must be careful that we do not become devoted to our work and make it all-important. It is perilously possible to become more interested in what we do than in who we are doing it for.

Martha, bustling about her business in the home, began to complain when she saw that her sister Mary was sitting at Jesus' feet and listening to Him rather than helping to get things done. Our Lord, with deep insight and understanding, quickly distinguishes between what we might call the urgent and the important. Mary, said Jesus, was doing the better thing – engaging *with* Him rather than just doing things *for* Him.

How easy it is to become more interested in working for the Lord than being with Him in worship. Don Bjork, a Christian writer, points out that the Great Commission was given to worshipping people. Matthew records, 'When they saw him, they worshipped him … Then Jesus came to them and said, "All authority in heaven and on earth has been given to me. Therefore go and make disciples of all nations, baptising them in the name of the Father and of the Son and of the Holy Spirit ... "' (Matt. 28:17–19). Unless we are closely involved with Christ we have little to offer to a needy world. It is so easy, as multitudes of Christian workers have found to their cost, to become more taken up with the work of God than with God Himself, more enamoured with the cause of Christ than with Christ Himself. Be careful that you do not allow the urgent to crowd out the important. Nothing is more important than spending time with Him in prayer.

Worship – repentant praise

The story in Luke 17:11–19 is astonishing: ten lepers were healed by Jesus but only one returned to give thanks! From this incident in the life of our Lord it is possible for us to draw a number of lessons.

Being 'cleansed' from our sin is, of course, the basic requirement in order to connect with God, but we must never forget the purpose for which we are cleansed – to give Him worship and praise.

When one of the ten lepers 'saw he was healed' he realised the extraordinary miracle that had occurred and wanted to give the Lord thanks for it. He alone, we are told, turned round, came back, praised God, and threw himself at Jesus' feet to show his appreciation of what the Saviour had done for him. Only then, and only to this one returning worshipper, did Jesus say, 'go; your faith has made you well' (v.19).

At the risk of overstating the point (but can it really be overstated?), the goal of salvation is not that we are cleansed or healed but that we return to God in humble service and heartfelt worship. The great preacher P.T. Forsyth expressed it like this: 'The Christian life is repentant praise.' It consists of ongoing repentance, not in the sense of a perpetual wallowing in our guilt or sinfulness but in a continual *returning* to God in praise and thanksgiving. Worship is really regular repentance.

> 'The Christian life is repentant praise.'

Follow the pattern presented in this story and you will not go far wrong: keep coming back to God with passionate and exuberant praise ('a loud voice', v.13), with deep submission ('threw himself at Jesus' feet', v.16), and joyful thanks (v.16). We can be cleansed, healed, restored, forgiven, but it is not until we return all the way back home in praising and glorifying God that we are made whole.

A time now come

Now we pick up on the words of Jesus in John 4:1–26, in which He says that the Father seeks *worshippers*. The point we have been trying to put across in previous chapters is now made by Jesus Himself. It could be said that Jesus came to seek and to save the Father's lost worshippers. This one Samaritan woman, who had sought to satisfy her deep spiritual thirst through sexual fulfilment, comes 'thirsty' to the well. There she meets the One who has living water to offer – water that will satisfy her parched heart and end her relentless search for inner peace and happiness.

A new thought is introduced by Jesus into the concept of worship: we are saved in order to worship the Father 'in spirit and truth'. God is Spirit, and to worship Him properly we must be in a *spiritual* relationship with Him. To worship 'in spirit' is explained by George Beasley-Murray in this way: 'The worship that God seeks is not frozen to a sacred building ... or tradition but a worship which is living, the ever new response to God who is Spirit as prompted by and enabled by the Spirit of God.'

If that is what is meant by worshipping 'in spirit' what does it mean to worship 'in truth'? Well, it means much more than worshipping sincerely because it is possible to be sincere but sincerely wrong. To worship 'in truth' is to offer worship that is rooted in knowledge, in contrast to the Samaritan woman's ignorance (v.22). It is worship based upon the reality which is revealed in Jesus Christ who is Himself the truth. A new day has dawned, said Jesus. The time has come when no longer does worship depend on sacrifices or rituals. We are free to worship God anywhere and everywhere.

Partnership in the Godhead

We can only speculate as to exactly when the disciples realised that their Master was none other than God in human form. They certainly had good reason to believe He was greater than any other person they had known: the winds were obedient to His commands, multitudes were healed of their illnesses, and He was able to send demons fleeing with a single word. Three of the disciples once saw Him positively transfigured and overheard Him in conversation with people from another plane of being (Matt. 17:1–8).

The disciples would have been deeply impressed by the fact that Jesus could bring the dead back to life and offer people the forgiveness of their sins. And, as some teachers of the law so rightly remarked, 'Who can forgive sins but God alone?' (Mark 2:7). On one occasion He said, 'Anyone who has seen me has seen the Father' (John 14:9), then another time, 'I and the Father are one' (John 10:30). Did the full weight of who He was really dawn on them while He walked with them in the Galilean and Judean hills?

Some think a complete understanding of who He was came only after the resurrection. Perhaps, oddly enough, it was Thomas who showed that he realised more clearly than the others that Jesus was not merely a mortal adopted to divinity when He said, 'My Lord and my God.' Did Thomas mean by 'God' all that we mean when we use that term? Surely it must have been so.

Suddenly Thomas came to see that there is partnership in the Godhead, that in worshipping the Son He was worshipping One who was equal to the Father. If Jesus was not God His integrity would have led Him to say to Thomas, 'I am not who you say I am.' The fact He did not is yet another great testimony to the truth of His deity.

Communion thanksgiving

'The Lord Jesus ... took bread, *and when he had given thanks,* he broke it ...' (1 Cor. 11:23–24, my italics). How remarkable these words are. When they were first uttered, at the Last Supper, Jesus was on the verge of making His final self-sacrifice. In effect our Lord gave thanks for His own self-offering! In doing so He was drawing together important Old Testament threads, for thanksgiving in Israel was expressed not only through public praise but through sacrificial offering (cf. Lev. 7:12; Psa. 50:23). The ultimate 'thank offering' – and the final sin offering – was the offering of the Lord Jesus Christ to His Father on the altar of the cross.

Not surprisingly, it is from the Greek word for 'giving thanks' (*eucharisteo*) that we derive the term for our commemoration of His sacrifice – 'the Eucharist'. This thought of thanksgiving should always govern our appreciation of the Communion service. It would save us a great deal of controversy if we concentrated less on the elements (the bread and wine) and more on the actions involved. After all, Jesus instructed, '*Do* this in remembrance of me.' It is the actions which are significant – the taking, breaking, eating, drinking. And at the heart of this commemoration is the giving of thanks. The realisation of this might well transform our times of Holy Communion.

The Eucharist, or the Lord's Supper, is a celebration – a festival, not a fast; a resurrection feast, not a funeral wake. At the table of Communion we share in the Church's great out-pouring of gratitude and praise for the one great act by which Jesus hallowed the Father's name and glorified His Father's holy nature.

Further Study

Matt. 28:8–10; Luke 24:50–53; 1 Cor. 8:1–6; Col. 1:15–20

1. What inspired the disciples to worship Jesus?
2. How does Paul join worshipping Jesus to believing in one God?

Psa. 27:4–14; Acts 2:42–47; 6:1–7

3. To what did the psalmist give priority?
4. To what did the Early Church give priority?

Acts 5:29–32; 2 Thess. 2:13–17; 1 John 4:7–16; 5:1–12

5. Reflect on how Paul sees the Trinity working in our lives.
6. How do you connect your life to the Trinity of God?

CHAPTER SEVEN

'THE ECOLOGY OF BLESSING'

Ephesians 1:1–6; 2:11–18; 3:14–21

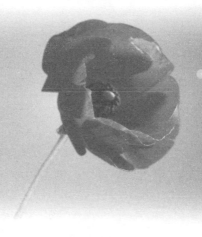

*'Now to him who is able to do immeasurably more
than all we ask or imagine … to him be glory …'*
Ephesians 3:20–21

Now that we find ourselves in the epistles we begin to see what is so distinctive about *Christian* worship. We can sum it up in one word; it is *Trinitarian*. The worship of the New Testament churches dramatically expresses their conviction that God is a Trinity of love – Father, Son and Holy Spirit.

Earlier we said that it was Thomas who first gave expression to the idea that there is partnership in the Godhead. After the Holy Spirit came at Pentecost all the disciples realised that love, power and authority are not the prerogatives of the Father and the Son only – the Spirit also possesses them and is a co-equal partner in what we now call 'The Blessed Trinity'. The great doctrine of the Trinity has not been fashioned, as someone has said, 'to make a simple thing difficult for ordinary people and thus help theologians to maintain their mystique'. It arose from the experience of the Early Church. The apostles said in effect, 'We have come to know much more about God. Now we see that He has a Son who is equal to Him, and that the Holy Spirit, who is also an equal partner, takes the things of the Son and reveals them to us. We cannot fully explain the Trinity, but there is no doubt that when we refer to it we are speaking of the central mystery of our most holy faith.'

Creator, Redeemer, Sanctifier.

From the earliest years of the Church the threefold blessing given in 2 Corinthians 13:14 has been in use.

We can never repeat it or use it enough for every time we do the expression deepens the impression: God is one, but one in three and three in one – Creator, Redeemer, Sanctifier. The Father in majesty, the Son in suffering, the Spirit in empowering. Once again let us adore the great triune God.

Completing the circle

The point we are to think about is one that we have touched on before, but now we shall consider it in more depth: our praise and worship actually blesses and brings joy to God.

The apostle Paul in Ephesians 1 launches a great outpouring of praise to his heavenly Father which begins with the words 'Blessed be … ' The NIV text reads 'Praise be … ' because the Greek word *eulogeo*, which means 'to bless', has been translated into the more general term 'to praise'. But please don't let this translation divert you from the point Paul is making: God blesses us and we bless Him in return! In William Hendrickson's words, 'Gratitude is that which completes the circle whereby blessing returns to the Giver in the form of unending adoration.' In their book *Doxology* Daniel Hardy and David Ford express the thought in this way: 'Blessing is the comprehensive praise and thanks that returns all reality to God, and so lets all be taken up into the spiral of mutual appreciation and delight which is the fulfilment of creation.'

Paul goes on to bless God as the Father of all the blessings that have been lavished upon us as part of His eternal plan (vv.5–6). You might be interested to know that in the Greek Paul's words from verse 3 to verse 14 actually form one long sentence. It is a veritable volcano of praise, marked by great intensity and effusiveness – the piling up of extravagant language that perfectly matches his mood of wonder and thankfulness to God. Paul is clearly beside himself as he reflects on the fact that all believers have been blessed in the heavenly realms in Christ. The simple truth Paul wants us to grasp is this: the reason why God should be blessed is because He has blessed us.

Relishing the blessings

Since Paul was an apostle of Jesus Christ, however, it is not surprising to find him, having given praise to the Father for His loving and eternal plan, then celebrating the fact that all God's saving initiatives centre on Jesus. God's sovereign will and grace are worked out in Christ. 'Blessed be the God and Father of our Lord Jesus Christ,' he is saying, 'whose eternal and heavenly will has issued in the historic events which occurred in Bethlehem and at Calvary.' God's eternal intentions have become saving actions in Christ.

God's sovereign will and grace are worked out in Christ.

That's worth a 'Praise the Lord' isn't it?

Let's relish the blessings that come to us from the Father through Christ. Bless Him for our 'redemption through his blood' (Eph. 1:7) – we have been set free because Jesus has paid the ransom price for us. Bless Him for 'forgiveness' (v.7) – that moral miracle by which our guilt is assuaged, the slate is wiped clean and, no longer condemned, we have new hope in Christ. All that comes from God and Christ 'the praise of his glory' (v.12). Bless Him, too, that all these blessings have been made effective in our lives by the Holy Spirit (vv.13–14). Every movement of the Spirit's work also contributes to 'the praise of his glory' (v.14).

This is what the commentators Daniel Hardy and David Ford call 'the ecology of blessing'. In this ecosystem of love, the love which flows out of God to us and back to Him again in loving praise and worship is the love that makes the world go round.

Abba, *Father*

True worship envisages every tribe and tongue and nation drawing near to God through Jesus Christ. What unites Jew and Gentile – those near and those far away – is the reconciling work of Jesus Christ on the cross. Jew and Gentile can now enjoy equal access to the Father through Jesus who died and rose again, and this is made effective in the Spirit.

New Christians often ask the question: Should our

worship be directed to God the Father, God the Son or God the Spirit? Worship is ultimately *to* the Father, *through* the Son, *in* the Spirit. This is not to say that we cannot ascribe honour directly to Jesus; indeed, we can and we must. Nor does it mean that we can never directly ascribe praise to the Holy Spirit as God; we can and may, when appropriate, invoke the Holy Spirit personally. It is, however, to say that even when we do give equal honour to the Son and to the Spirit we are, at the same time, giving glory to the Father (cf. John 5:23; Phil. 2:11).

Worship is ultimately *to* the Father, *through* the Son, *in* the Spirit.

Our sense of security in worship comes from three things: first, knowing God as our Father; second, coming to Him in the assurance that He receives us because of the work which His Son accomplished on our behalf at the cross; third, from Christ's continuing intercession for us at God's right hand. But let's not overlook the great work of the Spirit in all this. Paul reminds us in one of his earlier letters – the letter to the Romans – that the Spirit testifies to us inwardly that we are God's children, and this witness in our hearts causes us to cry '*Abba*, Father' (Rom. 8:15). In this 'magnetic field of the Holy Spirit' we can find ourselves being drawn to praise even when we might not really feel like it.

God's earthly address

Our praise and worship which, as we have been saying, is our response to who God is and what He has done for us, has to be offered through Jesus Christ or in His name. To understand this we need to consider what Jesus had to say about the Temple. Clearly our Lord loved the Temple at Jerusalem because on one occasion He drove out the money-changers saying, "'My house will be called a house of prayer for all nations." But you have made it "a den of robbers"' (Mark 11:17). Yet He knew that one day He Himself would replace the Temple so that people would no longer need a building in which to worship God (see John 2:19–22). He did this in two ways.

First, in Jesus' day the Temple was the place of sacrifice for sins. Jesus displaced the Temple by the offering of Himself as the ground of our acceptance by God. In David Peterson's words, 'Jesus offers the sacrifice that inaugurates the new covenant, fulfilling and replacing the system of worship associated with the Mosaic covenant. The pure worship He offers to God … is the only basis on which we can find acceptance and draw near to God.'

Second, the Temple was the location of the focused presence of God. Jesus displaced the Temple by His resurrection body. By the life which He imparts to those who are in Him they are formed into a living temple of God in the Spirit. In every act of worship we experience afresh the miracle of the coming of the risen Christ to be with His followers. Coming together in Christ's name in the Spirit we form 'a dwelling in which God lives by the Spirit'. Be staggered at it if you will but the worshipping Christian Church is really God's earthly address.

'Life at full stretch'

In Ephesians 3:14–21 we see Paul ascribing 'glory' to God and offering what we describe as a 'doxology'. This word comes from the Greek word *doxa* which means 'glory'. Glorifying God demands a leap of faith because we are affirming our confidence in a power higher than our own. To worship is to cast ourselves adoringly into the arms of a God 'who is able to do immeasurably more than all we ask or imagine'. This is why worship has been described as 'life at full stretch before God'. When we worship we are taken out of ourselves. We do not fall into a trancelike state but transcend our own thoughts and feelings and centre our souls on God.

Daniel Hardy and David Ford also say in their book *Doxology*, 'Our whole life is continually thrown into the air in praise in the trust that it will be caught, blessed, and returned renewed.' Once we realise how much God loves us and how completely secure we are in Him then we are set free to concentrate on God in thanks and praise. When this happens all sorts of growth and changes occur. However, they are by-products and not aims, and they flourish in our unselfconscious absorption in God who is the object of our praise.

In a doxology of praise we are lifted out of ourselves to the place where we enjoy God and are caught up with His desires for our world. Doxology, in the words of Walter Brueggemann, 'pushes us beyond control, summons us beyond our cherished rationality, rescues us from anxiety, transcends despair, overrides arrogance, strips us of self-sufficiency, and leaves us unreservedly and entirely entrusted to this Other One who cares for us more than we care for ourselves.' That says it all, does it not?

Further Study

Deut. 30:15–20; Rom. 10:5–13

1. How does Moses outline the circle of blessing to Israel?
2. How does Paul describe the spiral of blessing?

Lev. 26:9–13; 1 Cor. 3:9–17; Rev. 21:1–4

3. What kind of dwelling does Paul envisage?
4. How does John picture the new Jerusalem?

Psa. 96:1–13; Heb. 13:8; 15–21

5. Enjoy God with the psalmist.
6. How is Jesus both the object and the means of our doxology?

CHAPTER EIGHT

WORD AND SPIRIT

Ephesians 5:1–20
Colossians 1:1–14
Hebrews 9:11–28

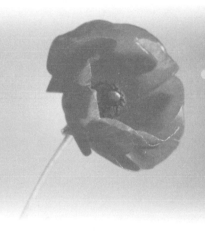

'For Christ … entered heaven itself,
now to appear for us in God's presence.'
Hebrews 9:24

The deeper we go into the subject of what constitutes Christian worship the more we realise how dependent we are on the work of the Holy Spirit within us to reach God. The Word of God is a powerful stimulant to praise, but so too is the Spirit.

In Ephesians 5:18 Paul urges us to 'be filled with the Spirit'. In making the contrast between being drunk with wine and being filled with the Spirit the apostle is contrasting life in the Spirit with the Ephesians' pagan past. Nevertheless, he is clear: the Spirit's presence is the needed stimulus for worship and praise. From what is known about worship in the churches Paul founded biblical scholar Gordon Fee has concluded that it was 'free, spontaneous worship ... apparently orchestrated by the Spirit Himself'. Dr Martyn Lloyd-Jones suggested that 'as the result of the operation of the Holy Spirit upon us, worshipping God is no longer a matter of duty, it is a desire'.

When Christians are open to both the Word of God and the Spirit, the Word and the Spirit combine in dynamic way, and this helps to account for the rich variety in worship expressed in what Paul describes as 'psalms, hymns and spiritual songs' (Eph. 5:19). It is not easy to draw fine distinctions between these three but we suggest the following. 'Psalms' may have been Old Testament psalms sung with Christian insight and understanding; 'hymns' may have been newly composed hymns to Christ; 'spiritual songs' were probably songs offered in worship at the prompting of the Holy Spirit, producing what another writer, James Dunn, calls 'charismatic hymnody'. Dynamic and varied worship should be the goal of every church – no matter what its label or denomination.

Total reliance on the Spirit

Look at Philippians 3:1–11. You may wonder what this has to do with worship, especially the parts which talk about circumcision. Well, consider this: we are able to worship God because we are the true members of God's covenant family. Paul's shorthand for this idea is 'circumcision' because from the time of Abraham onwards circumcision had been the sign of belonging to God's covenant people. So Paul is assuring his Christian readers in the church in Philippi that they are covenant people, the 'true circumcision'. In the new covenant we know the joy of sins forgiven, and because we have been forgiven much, we love much.

Under the old covenant only the priests were allowed to approach God, but now all believers can draw near to Him. Thus we worship with confidence and joy. Those who belong to the new covenant 'boast in the Lord' (2 Cor. 10:17). And why do we 'boast'? Listen to Dr Martyn Lloyd-Jones on this point: 'True believers boast in Christ Jesus, they exult. They not only believe on Him but their whole being is moved as they contemplate Him … they want to boast of the greatness and the wonder and the glory of the Person of Christ.' We do all this because we 'worship by the Spirit of God'. For this reason we 'put no confidence in the flesh'. In other words, we do not worship God because we are worthy to do so, nor do we rely on 'fleshly' feelings – worshipping only when human feelings are present. Rather, when we worship we are totally reliant on the Holy Spirit to prompt our minds and quicken our emotions to praise and glorify the Father and the Son.

> Now all believers can draw near to Him.

'Stop carping – start harping'

No greater joy can fill the human heart than the joy that comes from knowing we have been transferred from the kingdom of darkness to the kingdom of God's beloved Son. Our Lord's sacrifice sanctifies us and His Spirit empowers us to patiently endure everything that happens to us. Just look at what Paul has to say about giving thanks for this in his letter to the Colossians. Thanksgiving and praise punctuates almost every section of the letter.

We are to offer thanksgiving not grudgingly; rather, he talks about '*joyfully* giving thanks to the Father' (1:11–12). Since we are established in Christ we can bear the fruit of praise, because we are building on the foundation of Christ we can erect a house of worship, and as we are connected to the fountain of new life we can be 'overflowing with thankfulness' (2:7). Thus we need to 'stop carping and start harping,' as C.H. Spurgeon once said.

Gratitude is like a river that flows through and refreshes every relationship (3:15). When we are grateful

> Gratitude is like a river that flows through and refreshes every relationship.

not only to God but are thankful, too, for each other then peace will govern our lives and create harmony.

Thanksgiving transforms our prayers too (4:2). Nothing kills petition more swiftly than an unthankful heart. When this is the case then our prayers become just lists of complaints. Being thankful, even as we pray, strengthens our faith and lifts prayer out of self-absorption into the freedom of God. Thanksgiving helps to dissolve self-pity and enables us to 'be joyful always' (1 Thess. 5:16), not because we learn to play deceitful mental tricks on ourselves and praise God *for* everything but because, with the audacity of faith, we dare to praise God *in* everything (1 Thess. 5:18).

How *we worship is crucial*

Christian worship, we have said, is enriched by the Word of God and inspired by the Spirit of God. Both Word *and* Spirit are powerful stimulants for Christian worship. When Paul was writing to the Ephesians he emphasised the Spirit; when he was writing to the Colossians he emphasised the Word (see Col. 3:16).

Central to our worship as Christians is the message about Christ. Worship is our response to the gospel. As the good news is heard afresh we respond with joy and praise. Just as Israel celebrated the rescue from Egypt so we tell out the majesty of our Redeemer. We need to be reminded again and again that our songs and hymns should not be merely echoes of our feelings; they should be expressions of the truth of the gospel.

Paul insists also that Christian worship is essentially a corporate activity, hence the use both in Colossians 3:16 and in Ephesians of the phrase 'one another'. We lose so much when we individualise everything. Of course, only individuals can grasp these exhortations, but what Paul has in view is the shared experience of worship when Christians come together. The content of our hymns and prayers matters because worshipping together is one way in which Paul says we 'teach and admonish one another'. In some sections of the Church there is a great need for the content of the songs sung in the services to be richer and more biblical so that the worship is deeper in tone and substance. How we worship is crucial because we affect each other profoundly. When the full message of who Jesus is informs our worship from start to finish then every worshipper's life is enriched in the process.

An early Christian hymn

It was the experiences of the early apostles that gave rise to the doctrine of the Trinity. The apostles – all Jews to a man – already worshipped and prayed to the one Creator God. Then they met Jesus, and after His resurrection they came to see that He held the same status as God. At Pentecost the creative Spirit of God glorified Jesus to them so that, with heightened awareness, they came to worship both Jesus and God.

Martin Hengel, a leading German New Testament scholar, has pointed out that the high spots in the New Testament revelation of the divine status of Jesus occur in the passages that many scholars regard as early Christian hymns; 1 Timothy 3:16 is one of them. We could have cited other examples, such as Philippians 2:5–11 or Colossians 1:15–20. Hengel pondered how this amazing picture of Jesus as one with the eternal Creator God became known to the first believers. Perhaps, he suggested, it was while they were singing the psalms which speak of the coming of the ideal King, or Messiah, that the early Christian worshippers, filled with love for Jesus and with the Spirit, were inspired by the Holy Spirit to extend the boundaries of the psalms to embrace Jesus.

This sounds feasible, does it not? Didn't Jesus say that when the Holy Spirit came He would show His followers the truth about who He really is (John 16:13–15)? And when better to do this than when they were gathered together to worship? The Spirit will not give us a new revelation of Jesus, but He will give us a fresh vision of Him.

The principal worshipper

We look now at the book of Hebrews – a book in which the writer sometimes uses the Old Testament Scriptures in new and exciting ways to help us gain a deeper understanding of worship.

This is very evident from verse 12 of chapter 2. The writer takes the words of Psalm 22:22 and shows how they apply to the risen and ascended Lord Jesus: 'in the presence of the congregation I will sing your praises'. What a wonderful and inspiring thought. This one insight alone, if we consider it carefully, can transform our whole attitude to worship. This is what the writer is saying: whenever we gather for true spiritual worship, *Jesus is the principal worshipper*, leading us in praise! It was the famous nineteenth-century preacher, F.B. Meyer, who said, 'Whenever in the congregation of the saints there is an outburst of genuine song, you may detect the voice of Jesus singing with them and identifying with it.' How encouraging to know that when we come together to worship we are joining Jesus in His praise of the Father. But then, shouldn't everything we do as believers be done in the same fashion? Is not the bread that we break a means of sharing in the body of Christ? Is not the cup that we bless a means of sharing in the blood of Christ?

Are not the songs that we sing a means of sharing in the praise Christ offers? Are not the prayers we pray a means of sharing in the high priestly intercession of Christ? Is not the Body we are building with love and spiritual gifts a means of sharing also in the very body of Christ? Is not the love we share a means of sharing in the mutual love of the Father and the Son?

The divine Intercessor

The letter to the Hebrews is exceptionally helpful when it comes to understanding what it means to worship God. One scholar, David Peterson, calls Hebrews 'the most complete and fully integrated theology of worship in the New Testament'. At the heart of this is the wonderful vision of Jesus, whose life was one long doxology of praise to the Father, and whose death was the full and final sacrifice for sins. This perfect life and complete sacrifice is portrayed in Hebrews as the only basis on which we can relate to God and come before Him to offer acceptable worship.

What is more, Hebrews is unique in the New Testament for giving us the picture of Jesus as our great High Priest. Jesus is alive at the Father's right hand and there He mediates for us. He makes His own self-offering perpetually available as the means of our acceptance and forgiveness. He takes our petitions and the offering of our lives and makes them acceptable to God. Above all, Jesus continues to make intercession for us as

He pleads the merits of His blood on our behalf.

Pause and consider this: right now, as you read this book, Jesus is praying for you! That thought must surely stir your heart to worship and praise. Jesus once said to Simon Peter, '... Satan has asked to sift you as wheat. But I have prayed for you, Simon, that your faith may not fail. And when you have turned back, strengthen your brothers' (Luke 22:31–32). How encouraging that must have been for Simon Peter. Shouldn't the fact that Jesus is also praying for you, and knows the problems you may be facing, cause your soul to break forth in praise?

Jesus is praying for you!

Further Study

Psa. 119:1–8; Acts 2:22–36; 4:23–31

1. How vital was God's Word to the psalmist?
2. How important was God's Word to the Early Church?

Isa. 65:17–19; Zeph. 3:9–20; John 17:1–11; 1 Pet. 4:7–11

3. Reflect on a God who rejoices over His people.
4. How do our gifts lead to God being praised?

John 17:20–26; Heb. 7:23–28; 1 John 1:8–2:6

5. What is Jesus praying for us?
6. When does Jesus speak to the Father on our behalf?

EVERYTHING TO SING ABOUT

James 5:13–20
Revelation 7:9–15
Revelation 5:1–14

*'To him who sits on the throne and to the Lamb
be praise and honour and glory and power,
for ever and ever!'*
Revelation 5:13

James tells us that when we feel happy then we should sing (James 5:13). Gordon Fee said, 'Where the Spirit of God is there is also singing.' Throughout time the people of God have often broken out into song. The contemplation of God's goodness and power sometimes produces feelings so strong within us that they need to be expressed not just in spoken words but also in song. There are those who sing only when they are full of alcohol. Believers sing because they just can't help singing.

Over the centuries many of God's servants have continued singing even in the most desperate situations. They are what we might call 'unsung heroes' – unsung but singing! Gerhard Teersteegen, the eighteenth-century hymn writer, wrote of them in these wonderful lines:

We follow in His footsteps,
What if our feet be torn?
Where He has marked the pathway,
All hail the briar and thorn.
Scarce seen, scarce heard, unreckoned,
Despised, defamed, unknown,
Or heard but by our singing,
On children! Ever on!

William Law wrote in his famous *Serious Call to a Devout and Holy Life* that singing clears the air for meeting God. 'There is nothing that so clears the way for your prayers,' he said, 'nothing that so disperses dullness of heart, nothing that so purifies the soul from poor and little passions, nothing that so opens heaven, or carries your heart so near to it, as ... songs of praise.'

'A theatre in the round'

In the book of Revelation (the book that puts everything in its true perspective) worship is seen as centred on the throne of God. Throughout the book it is God's sovereignty that is being celebrated. The message that comes through in Revelation is that there is a throne in the universe and that the One who sits on it has everything under control.

The theologian Barry Leisch says that worship in the book of Revelation is 'akin to a theatre in the round' because the book describes a series of concentric circles with the throne at the centre. Around the throne are four living creatures who represent the whole of creation and the 24 elders who represent the whole people of God viewed as priests (Rev. 5; cf. 1 Chron. 24–25). Encircling them are myriads of angels so that the voice of every creature in heaven and earth is finally heard exulting God. The keynotes here are 'acclamation' as all heaven pays homage to the King, and 'adoration' as the elders prostrate themselves before the Sovereign Lord and cast

The One who sits on it is in full and complete control.

their crowns at His feet (4:10).

Throne-centred worship reorientates our lives dramatically. As Eugene Peterson astutely puts it, 'In worship God gathers His people to Himself as the centre. Worship is a meeting at the centre so that our lives are centred on God and not lived eccentrically. We worship so that we live in response to and from the centre, the living God.' When our lives are reorientated around the throne we recover our poise and sense of purpose. How it helps to deepen our understanding of worship to know that at the centre of the universe there is an unassailable throne and that the One who sits on it is in full and complete control.

'The Church's magnificat'

The sound of praise and worship echoes throughout the book of Revelation. Praise is given for the outworking of God's redemptive purposes and the certainty that God will reign for ever (11:15–18). There is praise for the fulfilment of all God's Old Testament promises which unite the believers of the Old Testament and the believers of the New Testament in one great song of praise – the song of Moses and the Lamb (15:3–4). Praise – with no vindictiveness – is also given for God's final judgment on evil and human wickedness, to which the saints respond with glad 'Amens' and 'Hallelujahs' (19:1–8). Such praise is a universal song which extends out from the four living creatures (4:8) and 24 elders (4:10), through the 144,000 redeemed (7:4), that is, vast crowds too numerous to count (7:9), to include myriads of angels (5:11), until every living being is enlisted in the chorus (5:13).

And this outpouring of praise is a multimedia event! There is a rich variety of voices – those of the elders, angels, indeed, the whole creation; there are solo voices and vast cosmic choruses. Music is played on harps and lyres. Festal shouts, thunder and lightning, solemn silences, exuberant joy, colourful robes, rainbows, glittering jewels, and fragrant incense all have a part to play in the proceedings. It all constitutes what theologian G.C. Berkouwer called 'the magnificat of the Church triumphant'.

What is the reason for all this? It is prompted by the fact that God, in Christ, has made it possible for men and women to be cleansed from their sin and join Him in eternity. It's so simple, yet so sublime.

'Reversed thunder'

Our final thoughts on this theme of the worship of God focus on the remarkable passage in Revelation 8 (vv. 1–5) in which we are given a tantalising glimpse of what happens to our prayers when they reach heaven. The language, of course, is highly symbolic. John discovers through a vivid picture a wonderfully comforting truth: the 'prayers of the saints' (8:4) are vitally important. When we pray our prayers do get through! In fact, the prayers of all the saints are vital ingredients in heaven's worship.

Our prayers, we are told, ascend to the throne of God, and are included in heaven's symphony of sound. In his vision John sees that every prayer is gathered up by an angel who mixes them with

When we pray our prayers do get through!

incense (signifying their purification) and fire (signifying energy). Then, moving to the ramparts of heaven, the angel hurls them back down to earth! They impact the earth with tremendous noise, accompanied by an earthquake and lightning. George Herbert, the seventeenth-century Christian poet, described this in a brilliant phrase as 'reversed thunder'. Prayer, which has ascended 'unnoticed', descends to earth with a crash – arriving with unmistakable and powerful effect. Offered to God as fragrant incense, prayer re-enters the world as divine action! Indeed, our prayers are a means of bringing about the judgments of God.

How encouraging and spiritually uplifting it is to know that what ascends to God in heaven from the hearts and lips of His children here on earth is integrated into the cosmic purposes of God. If our prayers count there then surely they should matter more to us here.

'All things new'

Finally we consider once again Revelation 5. Verse 12 tells us that all praise in heaven flows to the throne of the one Creator God and to Jesus, the Lamb of God, who shares His sovereignty. And so it should.

John weeps because the scroll of God's redemptive plans for the world is sealed. His weeping sums up all the laments which we saw were uttered by the saints of the Old Testament, and expresses the anguished cries of the martyrs. From this one thing is clear: all the unanswered questions thrown up by the ambiguities of history, all our prayers of lament and pain, of submission and disappointment, of grief and bewilderment, do indeed find their way into heaven.

In Christ everything is new.

The Lamb, however, is worthy to unlock this scroll that resolves all enigmas; the Lamb, by His own sacrifice, brings resolution to the disharmonies of a broken and discordant world. Now no doubt remains as to His divine place – He shares full and equal honours with the one personal God who created the world, and shares also in the sevenfold fullness of God's Spirit in power (v.12). He is all that God is, and He unfolds God's redemptive purposes, gives grace to meet all possible eventualities, executes judgment and righteousness, and brings in salvation's final consummation.

A 'new song' is sung (v.9) because in Christ

everything is new. Through Him we receive a new heart, a new spirit, and when we arrive in heaven we will be given a new name. Thus He fulfils His great and glorious promise 'Behold, I make all things new' (21:5, NKJV).

Further Study

Psa. 93:1–5; 1 Tim. 1:12–17; Heb. 8:1–6; Rev. 19:5–10

1. Why does Paul give honour to the King?
2. What worship comes from the throne?

2 Chron. 7:1–10; Luke 1:46–55

3. What various forms of worship were used in Solomon's Temple?
4. What reasons does Mary give for her personal magnificat?

Psa. 40:1–10; Heb. 3:1–6; Rev. 22:1–5; 12–13

5. What new song does the psalmist sing?
6. How is Jesus the focus and centre of all our worship?

NATIONAL DISTRIBUTORS

UK: (and countries not listed below)
CWR, Waverley Abbey House, Waverley Lane, Farnham, Surrey GU9 8EP.
Tel: (01252) 784700 Outside UK +44 1252 784700

AUSTRALIA: CMC Australasia, PO Box 519, Belmont, Victoria 3216.
Tel: (03) 5241 3288

CANADA: Cook Communications Ministries, PO Box 98, 55 Woodslee
Avenue, Paris, Ontario. Tel: 1800 263 2664

GHANA: Challenge Enterprises of Ghana, PO Box 5723, Accra.
Tel: (021) 222437/223249 Fax: (021) 226227

HONG KONG: Cross Communications Ltd, 1/F, 562A Nathan Road,
Kowloon. Tel: 2780 1188 Fax: 2770 6229

INDIA: Crystal Communications, 10-3-18/4/1, East Marredpalli,
Secunderabad – 500026, Andhra Pradesh. Tel/Fax: (040) 27737145

KENYA: Keswick Books and Gifts Ltd, PO Box 10242, Nairobi.
Tel: (02) 331692/226047 Fax: (02) 728557

MALAYSIA: Salvation Book Centre (M) Sdn Bhd, 23 Jalan SS 2/64, 47300
Petaling Jaya, Selangor. Tel: (03) 78766411/78766797
Fax: (03) 78757066/78756360

NEW ZEALAND: CMC Australasia, PO Box 36015, Lower Hutt.
Tel: 0800 449 408 Fax: 0800 449 049

NIGERIA: FBFM, Helen Baugh House, 96 St Finbarr's College Road,
Akoka, Lagos. Tel: (01) 7747429/4700218/825775/827264

PHILIPPINES: OMF Literature Inc, 776 Boni Avenue, Mandaluyong City.
Tel: (02) 531 2183 Fax: (02) 531 1960

SINGAPORE: Armour Publishing Pte Ltd, Block 203A Henderson Road,
11–06 Henderson Industrial Park, Singapore 159546. Tel: 6 276 9976
Fax: 6 276 7564

SOUTH AFRICA: Struik Christian Books, 80 MacKenzie Street, PO Box
1144, Cape Town 8000. Tel: (021) 462 4360 Fax: (021) 461 3612

SRI LANKA: Christombu Books, 27 Hospital Street, Colombo 1.
Tel: (01) 433142/328909

TANZANIA: CLC Christian Book Centre, PO Box 1384, Mkwepu Street,
Dar es Salaam. Tel/Fax (022) 2119439

USA: Cook Communications Ministries, PO Box 98, 55 Woodslee Avenue,
Paris, Ontario, Canada. Tel: 1800 263 2664

ZIMBABWE: Word of Life Books, Shop 4, Memorial Building, 35 S Machel
Avenue, Harare. Tel: (04) 781305 Fax: (04) 774739

For email addresses, visit the CWR website: www.cwr.org.uk

CWR is a registered charity – number 294387

Day and Residential Courses
Counselling Training
Leadership Development
Biblical Study Courses
Regional Seminars
Ministry to Women
Daily Devotionals
Books and Videos
Conference Centre

Trusted all Over the World

CWR HAS GAINED A WORLDWIDE reputation as a centre of excellence for Bible-based training and resources. From our headquarters at Waverley Abbey House, Farnham, England, we have been serving God's people for 40 years with a vision to help apply God's Word to everyday life and relationships. The daily devotional *Every Day with Jesus* is read by over three-quarters of a million people in more than 150 countries, and our unique courses in biblical studies and pastoral care are respected all over the world. Waverley Abbey House provides a conference centre in a tranquil setting.

For free brochures on our seminars and courses, conference facilities, or a catalogue of CWR resources, please contact us at the following address.
CWR, Waverley Abbey House, Waverley Lane, Farnham, Surrey GU9 8EP, UK

Telephone: +44 (0)1252 784700
Email: mail@cwr.org.uk
Website: www.cwr.org.uk

CRUSADE FOR WORLD REVIVAL
Applying God's Word to everyday life and relationships

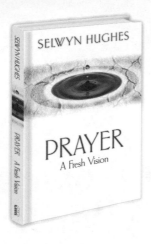

Prayer – A Fresh Vision

This book will encourage you to take a fresh look at your prayer life and teach you how to offer effective prayers that touch the heart of God and keep you in His will. Don't miss talking with your Father in heaven; learn the essentials of effective prayer: worship and adoration, thanksgiving and praise, petition and intercession, listening and confession.

£6.99 (plus p&p)
ISBN: 1-85345-308-0

The Holy Spirit, Our Counsellor

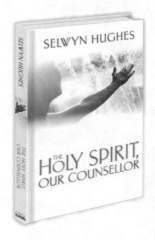

Focusing on the Holy Spirit, 'the Counsellor' who will never leave us, Selwyn Hughes writes of His role in our lives. The Holy Spirit lives in us and brings transformation. A book to encourage us to go straight to Him for our 'counselling' needs and open ourselves up to His life-changing power.

£6.99 (plus p&p)
ISBN: 1-85345-309-9